T0152113

HARD NIGHT

HARD NIGHT

Christian Wiman

COPPER CANYON PRESS

Cover art: Nathan Oliviera, *Man Walking*, 1958, oil on canvas,
60 ⅛ x 48 ⅛ inches. Hirshhorn Museum and Sculpture Garden, Smithsonian
Institution, Gift of Joseph H. Hirshhorn, 1966. Photo by Lee Stalsworth.

Copper Canyon Press is in residence at Fort Worden State Park in Port
Townsend, Washington, under the auspices of Centrum Foundation.
Centrum is a gathering place for artists and creative thinkers from around
the world, students of all ages and backgrounds, and audiences seeking
extraordinary cultural enrichment.

LIBRARY OF CONGRESS CATALOGING-IN-PUBLICATION DATA
Wiman, Christian, 1966–
  Hard night / by Christian Wiman.
     p. cm.
  ISBN 978-155659-220-1 (pbk. : alk. paper)
  I. Title.
  PS3573.I47843H37 2005
  811'.54—dc22
                                        2004022950

COPPER CANYON PRESS
Post Office Box 271
Port Townsend, Washington 98368
www.coppercanyonpress.org

ACKNOWLEDGMENTS

I am grateful to the editors of the following magazines, in which some of these poems first appeared: *At Length, The Atlantic Monthly, Critical Quarterly, Grand Street, Heat, The Nebraska Review, The New Criterion, The New England Review, Poetry Daily, The Sewanee Review, Slate, Southern Review, 32 Poems, The Threepenny Review, TriQuarterly,* and *Verse Daily.*

"Outer Banks (I)" appeared as a limited edition broadside produced by the Poetry Center of Chicago.

I am also very grateful to Lynchburg College in Virginia, and in particular to Thomas Allen, for giving me three years as a Visiting Scholar. This book would not have been possible without the time that position afforded.

for Naeem Murr

CONTENTS

PART ONE

Sweet Nothing

Built or torn away?
All I know is noise
of wood and workmen
woke me this morning
and for an hour or more
I've drowsed between
my body and next door
where a ladder scrapes
across the pavement,
tools clatter and whine,
tick, tick as someone climbs.
Time to get up.
Time to sit down
and try once more to work.
Time for Rebecca, the art
restorer from England,
with freckled cheeks
and fingers finer
than a watchmaker's,
who never sleeps
and lives on cigarettes, gin,
and Chinese food,
to stir upstairs, begin
the early ablutions
that have made these weeks
of fog and idle solitude
oddly intimate:
creak of bedsprings,
creak of hardwood,
stuck doors and drawers
and the rusty sound
of faucets coughing on,
water quicksilvering down

white shoulders and thighs
into the pipes around
me like a teasing dream
of rain; and the silence then
as she chooses what to wear:
the pale blouse
with its paler plunge,
the flaxen dress
that matches her hair;
click, click of her heels
over the floor, out the door,
up Clayton Street.

But not yet, not quite yet...
I close my eyes and let
myself recede again
into the pillows and sheets,
inflections and directives
in a language I can't place,
pink hues and pigments
of Rebecca's face
at my door last night
as she smiled, or tried to,
held out her fine-boned hand
the streetlight seemed
to shine through, and said,
"It's time we met."

The salt fog poured
off the water as we walked,
formed and tore
Sutro Tower, the bridge's
blinking girders
into the moldy keeps
and closes of Suffolk,
cathedraled Cambridge,

Rotterdam and Rome
and the huge high-ceilinged rooms
of the dream she'd had for years,
our footsteps echoing
through that empty opulence
of silence and chandeliers,
nothing on the walls,
nothing in the doorways
or in the long white halls
but the guards, gray,
impassive, motioning us on.

Up Parnassus, past
the hospital, where the Richmond
glittered between the park
and the farther darkness
of the bay, we came into the last
room of her dream,
immense, immaculate,
with guns of every kind
and time arranged
on the floor, all the gleam
and lovely grain
of barrel and stock,
trigger and hammer
hoarding the light,
as one by one the guards
with their sensible shoes
and saintlike patience,
their tired, proprietary
silence, pressed close,
waiting for her to choose
the proper moment
and means of dying.

It all runs together now,
her Catholic girls' school

and the famous cloud
she wiped away
with the wrong solvent;
the erstwhile fiancé
for whom she'd felt a long
elegiacal tenderness
in lieu of love
and John Constable,
of Suffolk, who thought
no ambition too high
for the plain stiles and stumps
of that place, no feeling
too intense or complex
for its mossed waterwheels
and random hayricks,
its mizzling, mortared sky.
"What in the world,"
an acolyte asked, "did you mix
these colors with?"
"Brains," Constable's reply.

How lovely her laughter,
unguarded, delighted,
as if her own mind
and what it contained
had surprised her,
as when, crossing Ninth,
linking her arm in mine,
from deep in the dream
she suddenly recited,
"Largo Star,
Long-barreled Luger,
Rast-Gasser revolver,
Parabellum Beretta,
American Savage."
And how subdued,

almost confused she became
in the moment just after,
her arm drawn back,
the guards near, circumspect,
and a feeling not of fear,
you wouldn't call it fear,
exactly, and not dread,
but merely a vague anxiety
for the form of things,
deportment, propriety,
a sense that there may be,
Christ, some art to this.
Does one, for instance,
shoot oneself in the head?
Blow open the heart?
Take between one's lips
the cold barrel in recompense
for all that's been said
or left unsaid?

"You ask a lot of questions,"
Rebecca said somewhere
out on the Avenues,
with a look I couldn't read.
I wish I'd dreamed of her.
I wish that moment
before we turned back,
when we stood wondering
how far we'd gone,
had, deep in the night,
in the steepest, most
possessive hour of sleep,
flowered for me,
accumulations of quiet
at the back of her neck,
the base of her spine

touched into such
fugitive and minor cries
that to have heard them
would have been a kind
of ephemeral faith,
sustained in the mind
only so long
as the bones and dunes
of her moved under
and over me in the sweet
fruition of loneliness,
loveliness, need.

But no. Burkina Faso,
that's what I dreamed of,
a border that was nothing
but a line in the sand,
acres of empty space
and fierce infernal heat
in which a man
with muttonchops and a waistcoat
wavered and stayed.
"So happy a death," he said,
spreading his arms wide.
"It was more like a translation."

Is that a real country?
Silence. Are they finished?
Or can they be on break
already, at this hour,
me still half-awake,
the fog still feeling
its boneless, soundless way
along my one window?
One does grow tired,
tired of pondering

some problem of balance
or proportion, wondering
what's next, what's safe
to touch; tired
of coming into rooms
rain has seeped through,
the walls awry, the floor
buckling upward; tired
of matching grain
to grain, seam to seam,
to make some one thing
that will not, one knows,
in time, remain.

How lovely it might be
merely to drift through the days
for a while, telling
the barklike body
and windy shiverings
of the tree moth from the tree,
attending to the sticky feel
of a bottlebrush bloom
or the way a traffic light
will change and change.
How nice one night
to go all the way
to the ocean and back,
fall asleep with the fog
distilled on skin and hair,
wake in the arms
of a not uncomely
English woman who says
"Really, though, a line here
or there, the color off by fifty years,
who fucking cares?"

Creakings, rendings,
the crash of some last something
coming finally down...

O Rebecca, wry Rebecca,
with your furtive interiority
and your English teeth,
your country Suffolk candor
and vaguely tubercular beauty,
you are not alone.
Always that man appears
in a corner of the dream
and, without hesitation,
without a word or tears,
makes of his face an abstraction
of blood, flesh, and bone.
As the chute opens
above you once more,
Rebecca, sucking him up
into the ceiling, laugh,
because what else can you do
when walls dissolve,
a floor widens to horizon,
and all the guards,
quacking like ducks,
take out their feather dusters
and tidy up the sky?

Don't move, Rebecca.
It's late, but there is still time.
As the fog disperses,
as the jokes and curses
come almost
into your consciousness,
and the hammer's makeshift
useful music

is briefly the dream
it ends, stay here
one moment more,
letting the morning's mild
explicit light explore
the curve of one calf,
little ridges of ribcage
and clavicle, declivities
of shoulder and throat;
all the lines
and all the little pores
of your face, the faint
capillarial glow
of your eyelids,
which slowly open now,
Rebecca, sweet Rebecca,
as I whisper in your ear
Bougouriba, Kossi,
Yatenga, Seno, Bam.

PART TWO

Darkness Starts

A shadow in the shape of a house
slides out of a house
and loses its shape on the lawn.

Trees seek each other
as the wind within them dies.

Darkness starts inside of things
but keeps on going when the things are gone.

Barefoot careless in the farthest parts of the yard
children become their cries.

Why He Doesn't Keep a Journal

In the dream he burns his journals one by one
because the fire is fading, because the fire is there.
The first is full of days
he doesn't remember, a sudden furious blaze
scorching his hair and driving him back.
Impressive, but brief.
The second's better, himself at twenty turning into flames
that at the time he'd tried to be,
a decade later, and dazed
less by loss than by what he's simply given away:
cities, friendships flickering as he says their names
with what could be joy, could be grief.
By the third he's learned
to hold a moment as it goes, to lean into this burn
while the flames toss
and taunt the darkness, which recedes, and waits, and gathers,
        and rushes back in like a wave.
Now the loss is truly loss.
By the fourth there's not one page he doesn't hear,
not one word he doesn't bear
as it adds its vanishing to that roar
with its own tiny cry that could be pain, could be praise.
Ash of childhood, ash of accomplishment,
love in the air like ash,
on and on and on,
everything's in them and everything's gone.
Now the fire once again begins to die.
In the dream this must not happen.
In the dream he knows why.
There's just one more,
completely blank, its cover black,
which he's never had a reason for
but always thought he might need,

carrying it around the world to pack and unpack
a thousand times in a thousand rooms
like a little portable grave.
Was it something in this one book that would not suffer words,
or something in himself no word would save?
No time, no time. He throws it in,
and what happens next happens again and again,
a thousand times in a thousand ways:
he looks dead into the fire that feeds on nothing,
and nothing stays.

Poštolka

(Prague)

When I was learning words
and you were in the bath
there was a flurry of small birds
and in the aftermath

of all that panicked flight,
as if the red dusk willed
a concentration of its light:
a falcon on the sill.

It scanned the orchard's bowers,
then pane by pane it eyed
the stories facing ours
but never looked inside.

I called you in to see.
And when you steamed the room
and naked next to me
stood dripping, as a bloom

of blood formed in your cheek
and slowly seemed to melt,
I could almost speak
the love I almost felt.

Wish for something, you said.
A shiver pricked your spine.
The falcon turned its head
and locked its eyes on mine,

and for a long moment I'm still in
I wished and wished and wished
the moment would not end.
And just like that it vanished.

Outer Banks (I)

Rain to which I wake
Cold into which I go
Little song, little song...

And the coarse unkillable cordgrass
On the dunes, detritus
Too ruined to recognize
Bare shell that shelters nothing
Nothing tells
What it has undergone

The pelican plunges
And the water closes over it

Wind lays its blade along the beach
Leaving shapes the beach can't keep

Whiter than the gulls the morning

Cry of hunger
Cry of warning

Outer Banks (II)

This isn't the end but there's no going farther.
The sea breathes,
a swirl of oil in the water like a need for sleep.

Fetal seaweed, glintless seaglass,
a seagull wrecked in a dune like a plane.
The living cry out as they flee.

What remains?
One shell the waves won't take.
The intimate distance that it speaks.

The Funeral

It happens in a freakish early spring,
some little nameless place well off the highway.
From where we're standing we can't be seen.
How we've come to be here's hard to say.
It's lovely, though, the handcarved coffin, the hole
beneath like a shadow standing its ground;
the flowers, formality, and not one soul
missing, as if this town were less a town
than an excuse for funerals; this mute crowd
with its out-of-fashion suits and useless shoes,
the solemnity with which each head is bowed
as one by one, and row by row, they lose
themselves to a keen indigenous grief
that binds them cry to cry and tear to tear,
until its binding is its own relief.
To hear their prayer would be to come too near.
We're glad for it, though, glad for the heaven they hold—
we know they hold—like light behind their eyes,
and by their consolation are consoled
if consolation's what this feeling is
of having something in us jolted awake
like children half-rousing in a fast, dark car,
hearing the tires drone, the dashboard shake,
until it doesn't matter where they are.
And lovely, too, the singing when it starts,
out-of-time, hopelessly out-of-tune,
yet strong, encompassing, as if it came from hearts
that knew as well as loss what loss would be soon—
a stab inside of every dawn at first,
then a scent, maybe, a story someone tells,
and each day a little less, a little more lost,
until finally some dusk they find themselves
standing like strangers at their own dead pain,

without confusion, though, without bitterness,
as if within remembrance itself they sang
that to forget is also to be blessed.
It's over. A whir of gears, a pulley's creak:
the coffin clunks awkwardly into the earth.
Now there's some final ritual thing they speak.
And though it's cost us time it seems well worth
the loss, as like a huge black flower they peel
away from this death so different from our own,
though we can't say exactly what we feel,
and though it's way too late to make it home.

Still Life: San Francisco

The fog is the body it can't quite be
these evenings of early August,
coming together
                        and apart
in the peach tree's fist
of limbs, the ice plant's leaves,
center and remnant
everywhere it is.
                        How suddenly
it can happen, a room lose
solidity, the furniture permeable,
walls gone granular
as the light and nothing
intact enough to withstand
touch.
            Hard to say
the moment
it's over, what's left,
what's lost, all of night
inside.

Scenes from a Childhood

1.

Untouchable, the storm-cellar door, its tin a pane of fire.
Long into the dark it's warm.

2.

Little things live in shapes the stones weep:
blind worms, grubs like thumbs, roly-polies
rolled up in their stonelike sleep.

3.

The ant an aimed light cripples into ash
is lifted by the luckier others,

borne down
the eyeless socket in the ground.

4.

Light wind pricks light across the dark tank.

An engine of insects hums in the cattails.

A sandhill crane stabs its shadow.

5.

What hand moves the clouds?
To what touch do they come so slowly apart?

6.

It does not end, the dirt and the distance and the seared air.
Stare and stare

and even crows become the light into which they fly,
that pulse of false water where the world becomes the sky.

7.

Is it painful, the locust leaving itself?
Is that what in the briar of night they sing?

How hard to the highest treelimbs,
to the toolshed and shut doors at dawn
their likenesses cling.

The Last Hour

Lean and sane
in the last hour
of a long fast
or fiercer discipline
he could touch dust
into a sudden
surge of limbs
and speak leaves
in the night air
above him, inhabit
quiet so wholly
he heard roots
inch into the unfeeling
earth, rings increasing
inside of that tree.
Without moving,
hardly breathing,
he could call
out of the long darkness
walls around him,
a house whose each room
he knew, its hoard
of silences, solitudes,
doors opening
onto the wide fields
through which he moved,
breathing deeply,
unbewildered by the dead
with their hands of wind,
their faces of cloud.
Stilled and gifted
in the last hour
before the first light,

in the dark place
of his own making,
he could feel rocks
relax alive
beside him, gather
from a moon-raveled
river the pearl
curves and blue
fluency of a girl
his hands once knew.

He could let her go.
He let it all go,
desire and grief
and raw need
going out of him
moment by moment
into the mild
immaculate night,
love by love
into a last
passion of pure
attention, nerves,
readiness…

        Light carved
out of the darkness
a muscled trunk,
each clenched limb
and the difficult tips
of a plain mesquite
taking shape
over the hard ground
where they found him,
his eyes wide

and his whole body
hungering upward,
as if he could hear
and bear the bird
singing unseen
deep in those leaves.

Hard Night

What words or harder gift
does the light require of me
carving from the dark
this difficult tree?

What place or farther peace
do I almost see
emerging from the night
and heart of me?

The sky whitens, goes on and on.
Fields wrinkle into rows
of cotton, go on and on.
Night like a fling of crows
disperses and is gone.

What song, what home,
what calm or one clarity
can I not quite come to,
never quite see:
this field, this sky, this tree.

PART THREE

The Ice Storm

Then all one day because of ice
they couldn't make it down the hill.
Or up, James says,
dabbing at a spill
of coffee, crunching toast as if it had a spine.
But he could work, at any rate,
could concentrate
on that book he's been reading,
or meaning to,
the flu—
or was it famine?—of '49,
some smoldering fact
he's found in the cold ash of some war.
Gusting upward, lobes and nose on fire,
his whole face florid
from the heart attack
he's somehow never had,
he sways, repeating:
Oh, we'd get down just fine,
I expect, but we'd never make it back,
then goes into his room and shuts the door.

Eva's hours have nearer ends.
She heats the little disk the cat sleeps on;
chips, until her hands are gone,
the glaze off all the feeders for the birds;
then writes two friends
to thank them for the birthday chocolates they've sent.
The word alone makes her stomach burn.
Which is mostly what age is, she's learned,
the senses sharpening backwards,
keen to what they can't perceive,
when to be wise means mostly not to wish
for what you love,

for what you love is pain:
spices or coffee, gin
bringing the evening light into your veins,
good chocolates the grandkids ravish
like a horde of crows.
You stuff your bellies with tomorrow's ache,
she can almost hear him bellow,
nipping and pinching to make them squeal.
Hot water with honey, one coddled egg, dry saltines:
Oh, what difference does it make?
She picks up the chocolates, breaks
the seal.

————

He draws the blinds on a wall of glass,
winces at the glare,
drags his chair
into the bright crevasse
between his bed and bookshelf,
takes a deep breath of air,
and buries himself
in one of the early wordy furies
of William Gladstone,
never a man for minor keys.
Creak and tick of the burdened limbs.
A creak and tick inside of him
as he crosses his legs and then uncrosses them,
shifts his weight to ease
the stiffness in one side,
turns a page like a summit he has climbed,
and breathes…
Think of it—twenty thousand books devoured
in Gladstone's life, and of his own
enough to keep an army of bibliographers occupied;

a whole age and empire crammed into one man:
spellbinding crowds until he couldn't stand,
felling his million trees,
filling six decades' worth of diaries
because a life is owed as well as owned, time
a gift of which a good man gives account;
who would mount,
night after night, a moral, high-rhetorical siege
upon some poor Haymarket tart
in whom ruin
and beauty were one word,
then go home and whip himself for a sin
that, all the evidence suggests, never occurred
but in his heart.

———————

And has just one,
pleasure spreading through her blood like a single drop
of ink.
She scours the stove and countertop,
bleaches coffee stains off the sink,
cleans leaf by leaf
the emerald ripple and the paradise palm,
both mostly dormant now,
reaches high for the philodendron, huge since trained to climb,
and pauses,
remembering the calm
of constant motion that her mother was—
a beauty, men said, though it hardly seemed
a part of her, looking out of her own face
like someone on a train;
and remembering, too,
the child-high hedgerows
along the lane

behind their house on Paddox Close,
the slice of sky above
growing wider as she grew,
the little park with its central statue
(who was it of?),
which, last time she'd seen,
weather had worried
to a Swedish ivy sort of green.

———————

Emma Clifton, Elizabeth Collins, P. Lightfoot—
even the names of those women are there
amid the parliamentary proceedings,
bulldog scholarship, affairs
of state.
He lifts his hand like a weight
to check his watch, little trembles traveling through his bones
into the air
as through plucked strings
a sound.
Two hours until the final round
at Palm Springs,
with its hairpin fairways, lacquered greens,
and that great eighteenth in homage
to Bobby Jones.
What a character!—touring in his teens,
retired at twenty-eight
with nothing left to win,
at forty storming Normandy with men
half his age.
Even his death was rare—
syringomyelia—cane to brace to wheelchair
without a trace of self-pity, regret, rage:
We all have to play the ball as it lies.

How much of a man's revealed in how he dies…
Poor Owen, barely sixty, Dean of the College,
a decent book on Kant behind him:
two days of chest pain
slivering into a lifetime's knowledge
and all the old beliefs
come flooding back,
silly relics and rituals, griefs
you're born into, some guilt you can't even name.
"Ischemia," that's exactly right: blood lack.

———

Sweet pickles and white bread,
salted ham,
a soybean spread
that is his one concession to his heart,
two butter cookies, plum jam:
she clicks
across the polished floor
through motes that rise
and float like molecules of light,
pausing outside his door,
hearing the Mahler chorus to which he always cries,
plays *to* cry, she suspects,
as if even sadness could be planned.
She takes the knob in her hand,
sees, inside its shine,
white tablecloths, crystal cut fine
as jewels,
and, and… and a man
with American shoulders and vowels,
that face
so open it wasn't, like the ocean,
and that tidal way he had of filling any space

that wasn't taken,
the table where she sat with friends,
afternoons and weekends,
classrooms, boardrooms, lecture halls,
the very bodies of their children,
in whose broad limbs he seems to sprawl.
Was that what she had fallen for,
talk of golf, and Oxford, and roast beef
in that gray decade after the war,
that it seemed so safe
a fall?

————

There—where the strings go silent
and that woman's whole soul
is in her throat...
A home can have but one composer.
Wasn't that the quote?
That long ironclad letter Mahler wrote
to Alma, the most exquisite
woman in Vienna, who packed
away that cold contract,
her party dresses, and her own precocious technique,
and settled, if you could call it that,
into the role
of being Gustav Mahler's wife:
I am not happy, and yet not unhappy.
My ship is in the harbor, but it has sprung a leak.
But he *loved* her; and she is in his music
as surely as the God
he never quite possessed nor fully lost,
as surely as the daughter is alive
inside this song, whose life
it cost.

Gladstone also had a daughter die at five.
Odd,
not to have thought of that before.
And Mahler's sister's name was Anna,
and Gladstone's sister Ann;
and wasn't Mrs. Gladstone's family from Oxford, or near?
Oh, William dear,
she told him once, *if you weren't such a great man,*
you'd be a terrible bore.

———

Was that a laugh or a sob?
Mahler dies off
into the long silences, polite applause,
and weirdly reverential tones of golf.
This could take all day.
She lets go of the knob,
backs away.

———

He looks up as if he's heard a sound—
what was it called,
that late-medieval game out of which golf evolved?
He looks down:
O'Connor's on the second tee.
It must have started earlier than he thought.
Steady head, steady head,
that pro at Sea Pines always said.
James lifts one hand above his knee,
so palsied now
he can't keep his cocktails quiet,
as if every instant were a shock

his body took.
Think of a stake
driven through your skull into the ground.
California fades into some salesman fool
he mutes
to spend three minutes
amid the doomed midcentury debates
on Home Rule:
Gladstone, suicidally brilliant at eighty-four—
One fight more,
the best and the last...
He looks up to see a ball
that's made of feathers struck
with something like a gardening tool
and flying fast
toward what, in the moment before he blinks,
is a cemetery gate.
Hurley or *shinty*, he thinks
as it falls.
In northern France they called it *soule*.

————

Head bowed,
her face in pieces
on the table, she seems,
as she gathers and releases
a little storm of gleams
from her hands, to wield the sun she's in.
Nineteen fifty-four it would have been
when James's parents gave them these. Proud,
so proud they were—
of their heirloom silver, their tidy house, Michigan,
her,
whom they kept introducing as James's bride,

though she was nearly five months gone by then.
She draws the cloth between the light and knife,
freezes.
How strange—to feel a life
that is and isn't yours
shift inside.
After the first brittle exchanges that day,
hot dogs and crisps, tours
of their property, their church, James's high school
where they first learned their private awe was real,
his mother rattling on in that white-noise way
that women will
when silence, like men,
is simply one more thing to fill—
Eva had nodded, and smiled,
and hovered just outside of her own skin,
trying to feel
that life inside of her again.

———

The dogleg seventh. A tough par five,
the fairway pared
to nearly nothing at its kink,
ramping up to inkblot bunkers and a pulpit green.
O'Connor times a drive
so pure and powerful the ball becomes the air—
a blue nowhere
for a long moment on the screen—
distilling white on its descent
into the rough.
Straight enough,
the commentator says, *but overplayed,*
going on to praise the progress O'Connor's made
since that wild tirade

two years ago on this same course,
the midnight tabloid accident
in which he broke both hands.
The camera pans
the fairway and milling gallery,
probes a dense, occluded spot
under a tree.
As if a man could simply start all over,
as if you couldn't read one character
in everything he does.
What was it Mahler said of Alma's early love—
Even his music has a weak chin.
O'Connor, lost in leaves, eye on the pin,
scalds a shot
past every limb but one,
which, after a comic chaos
of ricochets,
trickles back exactly where it was.
The Perilous Ambition
was Bobby Jones's phrase,
which is to aim at what you were
despite the hazard you are in.

———

Anna calls,
the fifth time in as many days,
some childhood memory of a sauce
for pears;
thirty minutes later calls again
to chat about the ice
she's seen on television,
one brother's ruined marriage,
another's move across

the country, cutting a careful trace
around the silence
of her second miscarriage
in as many years
until there is no word that's not that loss.
A walk, I think. You too, Mom. Tell Dad hi.
Goodbye.

———————

This stiffness in one side,
the telephone ringing and ringing,
the damn birds racketing
as if it were spring—
he's up, listing a moment while the tide
of blood comes back into his brain,
a fine pain
needling through his chest and down one shoulder,
which is what he should have told her,
he thinks, with as much a smile
as he can manage, that pretty girl he stumbled into in the aisle
of the grocery store,
who had pink-streaked hair, a pierced nose, and swore
by acupuncture:
that his body had, in a sense, acquired its own.
Point by point he feels the pain withdraw.
Like a world disturbed in water,
his bed and bookcase, the centuries on the shelves,
the television, and his own unsteady limbs
waver back into themselves.
Gladstone,
he thinks, striding across the room,
that mix of filial relief and Protestant rage
the great man felt for his sister, healed of lockjaw

and tremblings by the knucklebone
of a saint.
He stops, so close that he can see
each nub and flaw
in the white paint
of the door.
He takes a deep breath, lets it out slowly.
What's one hour more.

———

Forks and spoons and knives.
Fingers, hair, face.
What survives,
she wonders, rising suddenly toward the window,
of James's parents' place:
the vegetable garden and the screened-in porch,
the driveway bumping toward
the blacktop, as they called it,
splintering into a million little nameless roads
through the countryside
that she and James didn't so much drive
one frozen night so long ago
as glide.
She puts her fingers on the cold pane:
the iron deck chairs, the railings and the ground below,
each least tip of every tree,
all wrought to the same fine fragility
of glass.
Where were they?
She feels a quicksilver current in her nerves,
feels it pass.
Was there some way
to have prepared for this—

the childhood walks; the first lilt and flirt
of a voice she hardly recognized as hers;
that kiss
outside her front door
after James had met her parents, the taste
of something, tea, yes;
and more,
Amherst, New Haven, Ann Arbor,
vast tracts of life like landscape glimpsed from a car;
even labor,
Lord, vise of time
tightening, tightening, tearing you in two
until that one pain is all you are...
—these brief gleams in the mind.
And who would guess
that as the years find
their final focus you're bothered less
by the dark that lies ahead of you
than the dark that lies behind?

———

But who'd refuse a healing for its source?
Up, up
the slick eighteenth a strong putt climbs,
rounds
the lip of the cup
so deeply half the ball's inside,
emerges
only to slide
all the way back down.
Tough course, tough course.

———

North, night, late, and the branches fraught
with ice as they are now;
first one owl
like an oboe in the upper dark,
low, stark,
then farther off another;
and how,
as the time between their cries grew wide,
they never moved,
as if what each one sought
was not the other
but the distance that the other was,
and cried
but to align their silences.

───────

He lifts his eyes:
a last stab of light from the icy trees.
Tomorrow this will all be gone.
The limbs will unclench, the ground give,
and the melt
from branchtip and rooftop tick, tick all day long
like a rain.
Why did you suffer? Why did you live?
Things fever out of their forms again,
and he sees, blurred
into the list of names on the screen,
the first golfer of whom there's record,
King James of the Iron Belt,
who died in arms on the fields of Flodden.
Live long enough and all thoughts go one way—
Gladstone, cancer hiving his face,
turning on that last railway platform to say:
God bless you all, and this place,

and the land you love;
Mahler, harrowed and honed by the fever
he'd soon die of:
I am hungrier for life than ever.
Even this muted Midwestern woman
purging germs
on TV brings his mother back,
her eyes emptying, her chest ripped apart
by doctors frantically massaging that starved heart,
which feels, he's read somewhere, like a seethe of worms.

———————

Let it go.
Let the silver lie scattered as it is,
dinner unprepared.
Let an hour go by in glimpses
of the old oak iced in light like a chandelier,
titmouse and sparrow,
a cardinal like a cut the tree releases
calling *what-cheer, cheer, cheer.*
What is the cry she can't recognize?
What time is it now,
a prow
of last light slicing through the deep shadow
of the living room where she lies,
opera on public radio,
while the cat purrs
into the warm crook of limbs it's found,
and the deep-water heartbeat sound inside of sound
is hers,
the kiss still on her lips
as she slips
inside after the last goodbyes,
where her long-dead father from behind his paper mutters

You can bet they call him Jim,
and her mother, later, even quieter,
Do you love him?

————

Let it go.
Let the dead recede
into their names,
effect lie quiet with its cause.
In the end,
what difference does it make,
another day in grains,
walls a gauze
through which fine, faint voices bleed.
It will all come clear tomorrow.
Let the ache
that feels like acid rising in his chest
as he lies down on his bed to rest
from what it seems he's just begun
be only that.
Let it be done,
if not for good then for now,
if for good then with grace somehow,
the screen
flickering with whatever victory or defeat
one can always read about,
evening intensifying inside and out
until there is no pane between,
his eyes becoming heavy, and all he knows
grown light,
as he lets them—*Eva?*—close.

PART FOUR

Reading Herodotus

Sadness is to lie uneaten
among the buried dead, to die
without feeling a fire
kindled in your honor, that clean smell
of cypress rising and the chants, heat
increasing under you, into you, an old man
whose name the feasters weep and sing.
Confusion is to be born
into a people without names or dreams
to whom the dead must come in the daylight—
brief faces in the clouds, traces of familiar dust
to which you cannot call out, of which you cannot speak
as in the light wind those losses are lost again.
Suddenly, and without sound,
a god comes back, easing into our lives
as if he'd never left, opening
to our opened eyes those carved arms
as if that touch could be a tenderness to us.
Thus a man, a king, who sees a strange tree
burgeoning from the unveiled, inviolate dark
of his own daughter's loins,
wakes in high glee, doom
gathering in his chambers like early light.
So a woman who all night long has prayed
that upon her sons will descend
the greatest blessing that can descend to men,
finds in the first light they will not wake to their names,
their brows cooler than the coolness of dawn.
No telling how she answers this,
if after seeing her sons disposed of
in the custom of that country
—corpses torn by dogs, birds eating out the eyes
to sing from every tree what the dead see—
she curses her gods and desecrates fetishes

or falls to her knees that night breathing
an altogether original language of praise.
No telling if a man might carry
plunder and his own unsevered head
from the man-sized ants no man has seen
to the sweet tombs of a city where the dead rest in honey
always in search of something farther.
Does some dream country come to him at the last
—in the flash of metal, at the height of his own cry—
as to the slaves of certain nomads,
blinded so they will not know their homeland,
the birds one day become familiar,
the earth assumes old scents and contours
and the very air is suddenly sweeter than they can bear.
They are gone now, swirled
in the dark earth with the ones who,
seeing their slaves go mad, killed them,
who are themselves gone, their bones
partaking of the same silence in which lie
all the dog-headed men of the mountains,
headless men with eyes in their chests,
men so immense their shadows were as night,
men carved in marble to whom the gods gave only life enough
to let them fall to their knees...
                              Close your eyes
just this side of sleep and you can almost hear them,
all the long wonder of it, the lost gods
and the languages, the strange names and their fates,
lives unlike our own, as alien and unknowable
as the first hour on this earth for a womb-slick babe
around whom the whole tribe has formed a ring,
wailing as one for what the child must learn.

Night's Thousand Shadows

1. DEATHBED

There is a word that is not water,
has nothing to do with heat or light,
is unrelated to any one pain
though the torn body tears itself further
trying to speak it.
                      There is a sound
beyond all the sounds that I have made,
the needs that one by one I've tried to name.
It burns clear in the eyes searching mine,
the lips beginning to bleed again,
her hand squeezing my hand,
pleading and pleading that I understand.

2. LIVING WILL

All afternoon in the afterlife
of little things that love,
or pain, or need could not let go of
I hunt for the will
that will let me let you go.

I am distracted and slow—
all the grainy faces
in old photographs, letters
from the dead, deeds to places
that are only air,

some bright nowhere
of broad fields and sunlight
that was my idea of heaven
one long afternoon
of clouds and steady rain

when you sat and explained
where a garden was, a well,
excited by it, the hell
ahead of you
just a brief tightness at your heart.

Outside in the yard, crickets start,
cry *here* and *here* and *here*,
night's thousand shadows growing tall.
And now I have it, formal, final.
I touch each keepsake like a wall.

3. GOING

In the hard light and hum
of the room to which I've come
to stay, I watch the clock,
and wait, and hour by hour
begin to disappear.
Movements, mutterings: the brain
darkens like a landscape. Pain
in the pale arterial hills
flashes and vanishes,
takes with it one whole year.
Cotton and killdeer, a cloud
looks down, something's happened
in the wellhouse, someone runs
through tall trees, breathe and breathe,
is it my hand you hold?
The fever climbs. You grow cold,
then warm, now cold again,
a hive of nerves in the skin.
Some glimmer breaks through
and I bend whispering as fear
like a wind shakes you,
I'm right here, I'm right here...

Midnight, moonlight gauzing
the walls, the iron and umber
of intensive care:
I watch as it swells and falls
the puttied scar at your heart,
and read each beat and falter
on a screen and match my breathing
to the breathing of a machine
to know this time as it passes,
each moment as it goes—
until, early, you shudder

and quieten, blood gases
begin to rapidly rise
and somewhere behind your eyes
I fall in fragments away:
a child surprised at his play,
encroached upon by air,
a shattered man near dawn,
something about the way
he holds so still, his hair.

A Field in Scurry County

Late evening, cool, September, and the ground
giving its clays and contours to the sky.
The colors swirl and merge and fall back down
and for a moment, as the reds intensify,

I am a ghost of all I don't remember,
a grown man standing where a child once stood.
It is late evening. It is cool. September.
Pain like a breeze goes through me as if it could.

Rhymes for a Watertower

A town so flat a grave's a hill,
      A dusk the color of beer.
A row of schooldesks shadows fill,
      A row of houses near.

A courthouse spreading to its lawn,
      A bank clock's lingering heat.
A gleam of storefronts not quite gone,
      A courthouse in the street.

A different element, almost,
      A dry creek brimming black.
A light to lure the darkness close,
      A light to keep it back.

A time so still a heart's a sound,
      A moon the color of skin.
A pumpjack bowing to the ground,
      Again, again, again.

Sleeping in the Open

The touch that for one moment seemed
Her touch recovered in his dream

Is as he wakes only the wind
Moving over his bare skin

And through the single towering tree
That seems to rouse, seems a body

Responding and subsiding now
As if the years had taught it how

To be both taken and to stay
By giving inward and away

Whenever stirred by a real wind.
Even the strongest of them end.

This Inwardness, This Ice

This inwardness, this ice,
this wide boreal whiteness

into which he's come
with a crawling sort of care

for the sky's severer blue,
the edge on the air,

trusting his own lightness
and the feel as feeling goes;

this discipline, this glaze,
this cold opacity of days

begins to crack.
No marks, not one scar,

no sign of where they are,
these weaknesses rumoring through,

growing loud if he stays,
louder if he turns back.

Nothing to do but move.
Nowhere to go but on,

to creep, and breathe, and learn
a blue beyond belief,

an air too sharp to pause,
this distance, this burn,

this element of flaws
that winces as it gives.

Nothing to do but live.
Nowhere to be but gone.

Done

Men living in the dark regard
of their own faces
in the night's black panes
pause finally as if for air,

and standing there
at desks or kitchen drains
are so ghosted by those spaces
they look into and are

that something in them goes hard.
They are their choices.
They are what remains.
And they stare and stare

until a man who had their eyes, their hair,
who answered to their names
and spoke with their voices,
falls from them like a star.

Old Song, Long Night

If in some night of which I'm now a part
You wake in fear of nothing you can name
And, as you ease from loved ones, feel your heart
Quickening through your body with the same

Obscure imperative that I once knew,
Reading perhaps the very things I read
In search of something that will comfort you,
Some evidence that once the quickened dead

Endured a darkness that seemed all their own
And steeled themselves to name and feel each fear,
Then with each moment you are more alone,
More anxious, more afraid there's nothing here

But rage to sing some peace they'd never be,
Which dawns upon you as it dawned on me.

PART FIVE

Being Serious

1.

Serious smiles a lot.
At least that's what they say,
His Mum and Pop
Trying to be proud
As all the nurses gather round
To squint into the cloud
Of little Serious on the ultrasound.
It's likely just the way he's bent,
The head nurse finally thunders
Into the awe and argument
Swirling through the crowd
Where someone mutters half-aloud
In all my years…

Serious never hears.
Serious spins and spins
With his dumb dolphin grin
In the best bed there is,
Where there's no guilt and no sin,
No child more inner than this;
Nothing to will
And nothing to want,
No body you both are and haunt;
No drug of disappointment
Or feeling that there's never now
(Or do these seep in somehow?);
No suffering the world's idiocy
Like a saint its pains;
No traffic and no planes;
No debts, no taxes,
No phones and no faxes;

No rockslide of information
Called the Internet.

Serious isn't. Yet.

2.

Serious hears a sound.
Not unusual, in itself, nothing to be concerned about.
Here and there there's been a shout,
A song he seemed to be inside,
The weird whale-calls of her gas.
This, too, shall pass.

Then it comes again,
And with a far-off force
Which a shrink less serious than he
Will have him dream is a drain
That all his impurity
Is slowly drifting toward
(*Down,* Serious says, *down!*),
Beyond which he'll be clean,
Feel no pain...

Then the dark erupts in a rain
Of blood and muck
He seems to mostly be,
Holding on for all he's worth,
Which isn't much, finally,
Little wizened thing
Plopping out to an earth
Where cries of agony
Dwindle to equivocal joy
(*It's, it's ... is it a boy?*)
And some clear world lies
Just beyond the eyes
You can't quite open;
And everything is wet,
And loud, and broken;
And all of life is one huge tit
You're meant to somehow suck.

Serious staggers to his feet,
Slaps himself harder than the doctor did
And says, *I'm fucked.*

3.

Serious is learning silence
In the way most children learn to speak.
Poshlust!
He gasps after his first feeding,
Götterdämmerung in his first dusk,
His whole body writhing with a kind of violence
As if the world had wounded him,
Words his bleeding.

Anomie, Deus absconditus
Drift into the air above his crib;
Accursed progenitor, quintessence of dust
Dribble with the pap onto his bib;
As day by day, and week by week,
Serious wrestles with this difficult gift,
Forgetting, which, it seems, he is on this earth to do.

Boob, ass, oaf,
Riving out of him like greatness going off;
Ninny, crackpate, clunkhead, gorm,
Leaving him gasping and bent;
Fragments, sheep, rabble,
All falling, falling from him
Backwards into babble...

Finally Serious lies there, spent,
Language like some immense ghostly mobile
Bobbing just above his bed,
All power of movement gone as well:
Useless little buglike arms, buglike little fingers,
This heavy, heavy head.

And now if there's something Serious can't quite taste,
Or if he feels too acutely his own waste,
Or knows too acutely what he can't tell,

He screams and screams
Until the world knows what Serious means.

4.

Serious goes to school.
Just try it, his Mum says
As she lets go his hand
And wipes a last glaze
Of doughnut from his nose,
And Serious, insofar as Serious can,
Does give it a good try,
Though it's hard to understand
Why they keep taking a break
From taking breaks, or why
They can't simply walk
In line down the hall,
Or what, finally, is at stake
In a game of kickball.

It's time to draw a tree.
What a relief to work alone,
Serious thinks, as he picks a scab
For just the right tinge of sky,
Breaks his sugar cookie
To make a place of stone,
And fashions out of bread
A man with a huge head
And huge, ruined wings,
Gasping at all the ruined things
To which he's tumbled.
And calls it: *Cookie, Crumbled.*

Oh my, the teacher says
When she walks by.
Those are interesting trees.
Serious closes his eyes and sees
As in a vision of doom
Himself drowning in schools,
A whole ocean of fools

Nipping, nipping at him
With their tiny, tiny teeth.
And Serious sighs
With a prophet's wisdom
As he climbs up into his seat,
Stares out across the room
And like a prophet cries:
You're all going to die!

The class is a tomb.
Serious, rigid, waits.
A girl in pigtails giggles,
Then another near the back.
And as if along a fuse
The giggling goes
Up and down the rows
Till someone makes a crack
About his coat and tie
And the laughter detonates.

Serious climbs slowly down
Into that inferno of sound
Which the teacher's shouts
Are only driving higher,
Packs up his lunchbox, his dignity,
And his copy of Sartre,
And strides with a prophet's gaze
Through all that derisive fire.
Only once does he turn,
Briefly, to look back through the blaze
At the iron fact of his art,
Smaller from here, but unburned.

5.

Serious loves his Mum.
And then he doesn't, quite.
It's that way with everything—
Baths and plums,
The blessèd silence of night.

Would you like to help with this?
His mother asks
As she rolls out biscuit dough
And cuts it with a glass,
Or folds the clothes
Still warm from the sun;
But Serious knows
He was born with a task,
And though he touches the clothes
And tastes the dough,
Serious says, *No.*

Serious stays in the bath
Until his skin is shriveled and cold,
Eats himself sick on plums,
Feels in the dark
The dark he becomes,
And cries out in the night for his Mum.

6.

Serious is older now.
He just is.
Thank God, Serious says,
For whom childhood, that stupid carousel that never stops,
Always had an element of disingenuousness:
The tristesse of lollipops,
The sham of naps;
Fools dandling you on their laps
So you can play horsey, which damn sure isn't serious;
And all that endless business
Of pretending to be curious
About the most obvious things:
What's night? Where's Mama-Cat?
What's wrong with Pop? Can God die?
Why, why, why?

To hell with that,
Serious thinks, as he sits incinerating memories
One by one,
Saying their names as he feeds them
Like photographs to a fire:
Here he is in a baseball uniform
Squinting back the sun;
Here in a blue tuxedo with a ruffled front;
And here, Lord, with pimples.
He pauses a moment.
Do memories *have* names?
And what, exactly, are these flames?
To hell with that!
Done.

Serious owns a car, pays taxes,
Contemplates a pension,
Has a crease of gray along his temples,

But he is young, young.
He develops headaches, begins sleeping badly, and relaxes,
You might say, into the constant tension
That he really always was,
With far, far too much to do
To look anywhere but onward,
Or to answer the questions of a child
With anything true.

7.

Serious isn't Stupid,
Though they go to the same gym.
Serious sees him dropping weights
Or picking his butt and thinks,
At least I'm not him.
Nor is he Mean or Vain,
Those chiseled twins
With matching boots and belts,
Nor Smug who notes their sins,
Nor Shallow noting something else;
He isn't useless Timid
Who no matter what won't complain,
Nor fat-assed Nice sweating honey
On all the machines,
Nor Self-Loathing who smudges mirrors,
Nor Whacked who licks them clean.
Serious isn't Funny.

Serious spreads his towel on the bench,
Sits down in front of his own image,
And Serious strains at a serious weight.
And never, not once, when he's seen
In myriad mirrors around the room
That everyone else is straining too,
Has he caught himself too late
And finished with a roar
And more strength
Than he's ever had before:
I AM NOT YOU!

8.

Serious has a date with Doom.
It's not the first, and seems unlikely to be the last,
For they get on quite well, Doom and he,
Share similar pasts
And similar ideas about what life should be.
It seems, in fact, that this might just bloom.

And what a relief.
After Morose and Mad and Neurotic;
After almost falling for Grief,
Who was so exotic
She made all the others seem tame.
Then to discover she even lied about her name.
And to sleep with another Serious! *That* was odd,
Like wrestling with an angel,
Though it was hard to tell from that rough unsated tangle
Which one was Serious, and which one God.

But how easy it is to be himself with Doom,
Serious thinks, as he puts the wine in to chill
And sets two glasses on a tray,
Who always wants whatever Serious wants
And always agrees with what he has to say;
Who doesn't need to hear that whole spiel
About "going too fast" or "needing more room";
And who doesn't probe and pry that long needle into his brain
—*What do you feel? What do you feel?*—
Until it's all Serious can do not to stand up and scream: *Pain!*

Lucky to be alive.
And if he still has no clear idea where she lives,
And never knows quite when she'll arrive,
Still, something about Doom feels right
To Serious, and he looks forward to their dates.
He checks himself in the mirror, dims the light,
And waits.

9.

Serious is a traveler.
Traveling broadens the mind,
The man beside him says,
His tray table down and seat reclined
Even as they're taking off,
And Serious, who has his eyes closed
So he can do what Serious does,
Begins to cough.

    What do they say, what do they fear,
    Is this song joy or grief?
    This is a man, this is a god.
    Who are you and why are you here?
    To leave, to leave.

The meal is over,
Which Serious declined.
In the shell-roar of the cabin
He eases somewhat, is surprised to find
He could almost drift away.
What line of work are you in?
He hears the man beside him say,
And Serious begins coughing wildly again.

    What is that smell, what was that sound,
    Isn't that ice on the wings?
    This is the air, there is the water,
    But what do you do on the way down?
    You scream, you scream.

How far they must have gone by now,
That old familiar world miles behind.
The man eats an orange,
And now he eats the rind.
He eats his plate, his plastic fork, chews

With animal relish his Styrofoam cup,
Leans over to eat bittersweet Serious too,
Who startles and wakes up.

> Look at the desert, look at the green,
> Is there an end to that ice?
> Here is a place, and here is a place,
> But what is the space between?
> It's life, it's life.

10.

Serious is married.
What a weird wind this is,
He thinks, so still at times,
Then stinging the eyes to tears;
And how he seems both more and less
Himself, and how it seems at once all of loneliness
And something he can hold.
Or is it he who's being carried?
He shivers, and reaches out for her again.
Or is it she who reaches, she who's cold?
What is this wind?
Where are these years?

11.

Serious experiences loss.
Just like that.
Flat.
Serious experiences loss,

As if he'd come to some sheer cliff
There was no way around,
No way to cross,
And found,
On the other side
Of a deep canyon, himself,
Experiencing loss.

Serious, when the man is gone,
Tells himself that he tried,
Tells himself that he cried and cried
For all he was worth
To the man sitting on the other side
Experiencing loss,
Who one day simply vanished, or moved on,
Or slipped off the edge of the earth
And died.

12.

Serious doesn't speak French.
This embarrasses Serious,
Because insofar as he lives anywhere,
Serious lives in Paris.

He feels the city stare,
Feels himself sweat, and shake, as he tries to wrench
The little that he's gleaned
Into the lot that he desires;
Feels shopkeepers look at him as if he were a liar,
Waiters as if he were unclean;

And feels, in truth, not at all serious,
As if he had a huge balloon for a head
And helium squeaks for a voice,
As if gravity could be merely a choice
He were making, and he might instead
Simply stop, let go, and drift away.

Finally Serious, opposed to epiphanies,
Has one he can't resist.
He *is* Serious, and to be serious
Is to know something utterly or not at all,
And to know, moreover,
That as you let your half-knowledge fall
From you, *it does not exist.*

Just like that Serious is himself again,
Saying weighty things
About the flowers in the stalls,
Pondering a splendid mirage
Called the Seine.

And if he wakes saying *fromage,*
Or in some shop feels

Right on the verge of translating *please,*
Serious knows it's a dream,
And knows from childhood what to do.
Point and scream
Until the damn fools give you cheese.

13.

Serious has some culture.
He knows some things.
And if, as he begins to speak,
He should feel the immense wings
Of ignorance shadowing him, that dirty vulture
That squawks in drawl and drips tobacco juice,
Serious knows what shelter to seek.

Pick a name and Bach is better.
Modernism was powerful but diffuse.
Life's drained out of pictures since the Renaissance.
Technique! Technique! Technique!
And about all that spastic flatulence
Called contemporary art,
Well, Serious hardly knows where to start.

Serious sits through opera without a yawn,
Chews up books on which weaker teeth would shatter;
He can tell you where one brushstroke lies,
List the reasons courtly love is gone,
Pluck the speck of subject matter
From Henry James.
Serious knows some things.

He thinks and thinks and thinks
Until his ignorance shrinks
To the tiniest of flies
Alighting somewhere in the Louvre.
Carefully, carefully, Serious creeps
With his massive swatter,
Saying, *Don't move. Don't move.*

14.

Serious gets online.
There's something he needs to find,
Something simple he can't quite bring to mind,
And which, apparently, his books don't contain.

It's like a collective human brain,
A brainless human once said to Serious;
And isn't that the truth, he thinks,
As fact unravels into fact,
All this wilderness of sites and useless links
You slash your way through because it's got to be there,
Everything's there;
Until you acquire a ruined-gambler sort of lean
And a ruined-gambler sort of stare,
Staking everything on just one more screen,
So far from where you started,
With no way back.
And what does it all mean?

Serious hits the button, and it all goes black.

15.

Serious pays a bill,
Figures nervously when the check will clear,
Considers all the little eddies of fear
On which a life rides,
All the half-frantic shifts and swerves of will
That all the while this current decides;

And how, amid such scrupulous thrift and pinch—
The red-eye flights and the lousy scotch,
Wearing bad glasses when your sight
Has worsened, not having your shirts laundered—
There's still this nagging feeling of waste,
This bitter taste
And this headache nothing seems to touch,
As if you woke after some long debauch
With only the vaguest memory of music, and light,
And something squandered.

Serious calls the bank,
Gives over his soul in code
To some approximately human voice,
Sits and sits and sits on hold.
Finally, no wiser, and on the brink
Of going under, Serious makes a choice:

He hangs up and pours himself a drink.

16.

Serious believes in nothing.
It's a nice day, what should we do?
What are you thinking?
What's been bothering you?
What's that you're drinking?

Serious spreads the paper on his lap
To confirm what's new under the sun,
Hears a *tap, tap, tap*
Against the windowpane.

Nothing ventured, nothing gained
Floats up from childhood like a bit of ash,
And Serious, pausing, can almost see
His old preacher, that atom bomb of idiocy
Who every Sunday would explode.
Still, Serious thinks, there's a truth to set you free.
But who could survive the blast?

Tap, tap, tap.

Serious skims the sports pages,
Reads about a storm that rages
Far out at sea.
Some talking dog is taking office,
Some country wiping out monuments, expunging its past.

Tap, tap, tap.

Goddamnit, Serious says, midway through a war,
And thinks again of that old bore
Who talked and talked and talked
Until you felt your head loll and sway
Like some huge flower on a tiny stalk
That one good breeze would break;

And how you'd see him afterwards eating chicken fried steak,
Chicken fried man,
With a tiny transistor radio in his hand
So he could listen to the football game;
And how his face seethed and writhed with what seemed pain
If he saw you coming to his booth,
And he stared off as if some great truth
Were finally, finally coming clear in that chicken fried brain
And like a prophet he was going to stand up and shout—
Until what plopped innocuously out
Was your own name.

Tap, tap, tap.

Serious puts aside the news of the day
And walks to the only window there is.
But there's no wind, not even the grass stirs.
And anyway, there's no tree.
Serious shrugs and turns away.
Must just be me.

17.

Serious sees a child
In the playground across the street,
Sees his huge stupid head and huge stupid feet
As he tries to keep up with the games,
And hears his sonar screams
Of delight amid the other children's screams,
And hears his timid weeping when they call him names.

Serious sees the child standing apart sometimes
Driveling to himself in silly rhymes,
And sees him pretend to look intently at the sky
If Serious walks by,
Or sees him simply stop and stare.

Gradually Serious starts seeing the child everywhere,
In a store standing in an aisle,
In the subway while
Serious is trying to work on the way home,
Or laughing with his family in a restaurant
Where Serious eats alone.

Serious knows the truth.
This child wants something, his whole nature is want.
And it begins to be annoying,
This novice cringing, all the imbecilic and cloying
Tactics of being cute,
The whole hangdog way he has of panhandling pity
With his freckles and his missing tooth,
Sitting all fidgety in his Sunday suit
Or babbling happily as he's leaking snot;
And then the air he suddenly puts on of being serious
When it's so obvious he's not.

Serious sees the child in the playground
Standing to the side,

Sees his face whiten and his eyes go wide
As Serious crosses the street and strides
Until his shadow swallows the child
And leans down close enough for them to kiss.
I don't have time for this,
Serious says,
I've got too much to do.

And the child says, *Who are you?*

18.

Serious kills himself.
No, no,
Shivering out of a dream,
Starlight and the hard glitter
Under the bridge's beam,
Serious, Serious,
Don't go.

Serious crawls out of bed,
Feels the cold in the floor
And thinks, suddenly, of lovely Mad
(Where can she be?)
Who'd bolt out of sleep and scream
Farmers get up at four!
It's three.

Serious makes himself a cup of coffee,
Which he doesn't drink;
Tries and fails to read,
Tries and fails to think.
Serious sits, and holds himself still,
Minute by minute;
Until the dawn finally comes
And he is in it.

19.

Serious lives alone.
It's better this way, he tells himself,
As he takes a pan from the pan shelf,
A spatula from the spatula drawer,
And fries two eggs the way *he* likes them:
Yolks of stone.

No more gnats of chatter over breakfast.
No more breakfast. It's noon.
No one prancing by with only panties on
When he's almost, almost broken through,
Or singsonging outside his door
Serious, O Serious, where are you?
No more!

But what, finally, *does* Serious do?
He sits, ignores the ringing phone,
Looks at a wall
On one of the last warm days of the year,
And settles back into the lifelong call
Of being serious,
Which is to see, within that whiteness,
Leaves being gently blown,
And to feel their colors as they fall.

20.

Serious gives a speech.
He sets his papers on the podium,
His glass within easy reach,
Tap, tap, taps the microphone.
How vast this venue is.
How absolute this darkness.

To be serious is to be alone!
Serious cries out with a triumphant look on his face,
Waiting for the echoes to end
Out there in all that space,
Which the words at once define and extend.
It takes a while, but they do die.
The spotlight lasers in.
He blinks hard, starts again.

To know in every hand another's touch,
To hear a silence words only intensify,
To feel not too little but too much
This attenuated world—

Serious begins to sweat,
Feels the back of his shirt grow wet;
Looks down to see his papers swirled
And scattered, the glass on the floor, broken.
What's with this fucking light, he thinks,
Or was it spoken?
He glares out at the dark, impassive crowd
And as if by force he could make them wake
Hears his voice growing loud:

Whatever you most treasure you will break,
Whatever you hold closest you will let go,
There is no place that you will not leave!

But to be serious—
          Serious says,
Quietly now, because he has them, they are his—

To be serious, to be truly serious, is to know
That what you call your losses you cannot grieve,
For it was never quite these things that you wanted
—This treasure, this touch, this one place—
But by such life to be haunted.

Brilliant!
No notes, no flaws.
Serious stands back and waits for applause.
The hall is silent, utterly silent,
The heat tropic.

Serious looks around, confused,
Turns to the man who introduced him
Then can't remember being introduced;
And even given his credentials,
This suddenly seems a most unlikely topic.

Serious tries to get out of the light,
But the light goes where Serious goes.
He blunders to the edge of the stage,
A cliff
Breaking off into a dark
In which there's no movement, no voices, not one sigh.
Serious feels the rage
Draining out of him, and feels a chill, and whispers,
Where am I?

21.

Serious nears an end.
It's cold and getting colder,
And Serious, older,
Sits outside thinking of his good friend,
Who like so much of Serious is gone,
And thinking of that godforsaken dawn
After the one night of his life he spent outdoors.

Tell me,
His good friend said
When Serious staggered out to the fire,
Which form would you say is higher,
Tragedy or comedy?

And Serious, who had stumbled full-bladdered
In the night from a dream of bears,
Then dreamed himself the object
Of a dozen hungry stares,
Who had swiveled, pissed into the tent,
And sworn such things it would take a life to repent,
Serious, exhausted Serious,
Was silent.

Because it's been troubling me,
Serious, that the answer can only be tragedy.
To be conscious is to be conscious of
Losing whatever it is that you most love,
And thus an art that's truly great
Will always have one deepest truth to tell,
Which is, my friend, this life is hell.

Serious looks at the sky. It's late.
A small wind blows
The trees, and Serious, shivering, knows
He should head inside,

That he is not well.
But sitting here, letting his eyes close,
Serious can almost see that lake
Aflame with the early sun, and smell
The sweet burn of that wood,
And feel the way it seemed his heart would surely break
Were it not for the strange lightness in his head
As his friend smiled and said,
But maybe earth is the heaven of the good.

22.

Serious talks to God.
There's no one else left.
His mind is mash,
His world is ash,
And Serious occasionally forgets himself,
Though he is not, *not* Bereft,
That sniveling idiot two doors down
Who sits up late
With only ashes in the grate
And talks to God.

See? Serious says. *See?*
Nothing.
Serious spreads his arms magnanimously
As if to give God the floor.
God declines.
Thou know'st the first time that we smell the air
We wawl and cry,
Serious says, louder than before.
And then we wawl and cry some more,
And then we die,
And then we rot!
Again he waits in case
There's disagreement. There's not.

Serious scoffs, goes to brush his teeth,
Forgets briefly to avert his eye
From the mirror's glare
And finds his father there,
That gentle baffled man
Who, when there was no hope,
When he couldn't even stand,
Carved from a piece of soap
A silly yellow duck

And set it in a little yellow dish.
Serious feels a tingling in his hair
And mutters something close to a prayer,
I wish, I wish...

The lights go out.
Goddamnit, Serious shouts
As he trips and falls
To his knees on the floor,
Banging his head on the door
As he tries to rise.
GodDAMNIT! Serious cries.

The lights come on.
His father's gone,
But there, at the edge of the sink,
Balances the little duck in the little dish
No serious person would ever keep.
Serious tries to think,
Steadies himself as if at some brink,
Decides he needs sleep,
That's what he needs,
Crawling fully clothed into his bed
And pulling the covers to his chin
Because, it seems, there's some strange wind
That's somehow gotten inside.
So unlike Serious,
To leave a door unclosed.

Yet here it is, gathering strength
As it blows his books
To the floor and it blows
Right through his body and it blows
Behind and below and above
And out of the whirlwind a voice cries,

Love

What? Serious says, as he tries
To sit upright and looks
Wildly around him,
Raising his fist in the air.
The things … I have lost—

Immediately he is tossed
Back against the wall
By the force of a storm
That has no source, no form,
And hears again the call
Out of nowhere:

      Love

My God! Serious screams,
Unable to help himself,
What maundering politician,
What decerebrated pop star,
What stupid puling poet
Couldn't tell me that?
Struggling to get out of bed
He starts to cough, then choke,
A riot in his heart,
A riot in his head
As he falls off the edge to the floor.
Who do you think you are,
He gasps. *Is this…*
Is this some sort of JOKE?

Suddenly the strange wind is quiet,
But no less strange the calm that comes after.

I'm serious, the voice says.

And Serious dies of laughter.

EPILOGUE

The dead man's famous.
No one now remembers him alive,
Or knows his name, or anything he did.
Still, a few stories survive
After all this while
Of a weird-looking man
With a weird-looking smile
That had, it's said,
Almost a kind of life to it,
Though the man was seriously dead.

And some remember how all the flies
Vanished for miles;
And some say no, no, but the buzzards had weird smiles
As if they knew something.
And some tell of an old woman
Who would come and whisper in the dead man's ear,
And smooth the dead man's hair,
And if the door opened, disappear.
There are even stories of that grim mortician
Who thought the smile undignified
And tugged and tugged so hard
He slipped and fell inside
Right on top of the dead man,
Whose lips, he swore, seemed to soften,
Seemed to somehow kiss.
And some remember this:
Before the lid was sealed on that coffin
And the nails driven,
There were on that face real tears.
And some say he smiled like a man forgiven.

The dead man never hears.
The dead man spins and spins

With his dumb dolphin grin
Through all the places where he is
When people talk of him again:
In classrooms or in planes,
In boredom or in pain;
In front of screens
Or in the spotlight's glare;
In days too mild to bear
And in the long nights where
The dark grows steep,
The wind wild,
And a mother rises from her sleep
To calm her serious child.

Christian Wiman is the author of one previous book of poetry, *The Long Home* (1998), which won the Nicholas Roerich Prize, and a book of criticism, *Ambition and Survival: Essays on Poetry* (2004). His poems, criticisms, and personal essays appear widely, in such magazines as *The Atlantic Monthly, Harper's, The New York Times Book Review*, and *Slate*. He is the editor of *Poetry* magazine.

The Chinese character for poetry is made up of two parts: "word" and "temple." It also serves as pressmark for Copper Canyon Press. Founded in 1972, Copper Canyon Press remains dedicated to publishing poetry exclusively, from Nobel laureates to new and emerging authors. The Press thrives with the generous patronage of readers, writers, booksellers, librarians, teachers, students, and funders—everyone who shares the conviction that poetry invigorates the language and sharpens our appreciation of the world.

Major funding has been provided by:

The Paul G. Allen Family Foundation
Lannan Foundation
National Endowment for the Arts
The Starbucks Foundation
Washington State Arts Commission

For information and catalogs:

COPPER CANYON PRESS
Post Office Box 271
Port Townsend, Washington 98368
360/385-4925
www.coppercanyonpress.org

This book was designed by Phil Kovacevich, using the typeface New Caledonia. William A. Dwiggins designed Caledonia for Linotype in 1939. In the late 1980s, Linotype released New Caledonia, removing some of the constraints placed on the original design when it was first produced in metal and augmenting the range of weights for the typeface. New Caledonia is one of the most widely used book types of all time.

CPSIA information can be obtained
at www.ICGtesting.com
Printed in the USA
JSHW020036311221
21584JS00008B/3

9 781556 592201